SUPERTRAINS

SUPERTRAINS

John Gabriel Navarra

DOUBLEDAY & COMPANY, Inc.
GARDEN CITY, NEW YORK

This book is part of a Museum of Science & Industry/Chicago series of science books published by Doubleday & Company, Incorporated. The series is designed to inform, stimulate, and challenge youngsters on a wide range of scientific and technological subjects.

Library of Congress Cataloging in Publication Data

Navarra, John Gabriel.
    Supertrains.

    Includes index.
    SUMMARY: Discusses high-speed trains, aerotrains, monorails, and tube trains for passenger travel and their implications for environmental quality and new designs for living.
    1. Railroads—Juvenile literature. [1. Railroads]
I. Title.
TF148.N38   385'.09'047
ISBN 0-385-01940-8 Trade
    0-385-02024-4 Prebound
Library of Congress Catalog Card Number 74–18820

Preface

Most people seem to be going someplace all the time. They travel to work, school, shop, play, and visit friends. We are constantly on the move.

Ground transportation systems in most regions are not adequate. The public wants and deserves short travel times, brief waiting periods, safety, convenience, and comfort. Today, there are other requirements, too: We must conserve fuel, reduce environmental pollution, preserve the countryside, and beautify the cities.

We are learning that our transportation needs can only be met by using every mode of travel to best advantage. For more than thirty years we have neglected the tracked vehicles called *trains*. In this book you will find some information about the role of tracked vehicles in solving our transportation problems.

The progress made by a society is closely linked with the development of its transportation systems. As you read, keep this question in mind: What kind of progress are we making?

JOHN GABRIEL NAVARRA

Contents

UNIT 1

Rethinking Mass Transit

Almost every industrialized country is worried about its oil supplies and pollution. The search is on for ways to use less fuel and to reduce pollution.

One way of meeting the energy crisis is by reviving the one-time glory of the train. A Boeing 707 airplane, for example, uses about five times more fuel than a gas-turbo train carrying the same number of passengers the same distance. Trains are the most economical form of transportation we have.

A train—carrying hundreds of passengers—helps with the pollution problem, too. In the United States during 1974, automobiles were responsible for 47 per cent of the air pollution. Watch a major highway on a business day. Each automobile puts out its share of poisonous fumes. And most of the cars carry only one person, the driver!

1

In Great Britain

Great Britain's shift in transportation emphasis from *roads* to *rails* has been going on for some time. The British Government has asked companies to study their transport needs very carefully. The companies are being urged to ship more things by rail and less by highway.

Uncertain oil supplies are part of the reason for the British shift from roads to rails. But there is another reason, too. The British public resents the amount of land that has been destroyed to build highways. The citizens of Great Britain feel that too much land has been "grabbed" by the highway builders.

During the 1960s, the British Railways Board began studies of ways to improve rail service. They concluded that most railways must use the track they already have along with the crossings and sharp bends. British Railways developed an Advanced Passenger Train, called *APT*, which uses their existing track and signaling equipment.

The APT of Great Britain is driven by gas turbines. In the photograph of the APT below, there is a power car at both ends with two passenger cars in between. This particular APT has the same weight and seating capacity of a Boeing 747 airliner. A comparison of the train and plane gives a certain advantage to the train in these days of an energy crisis. The train uses a lot less fuel than the plane for each passenger mile traveled.

A railway wheel set consists of two flanged wheels joined to an axle. Steel wheels running on two steel rails are at the heart of traditional railroading. The flanged wheels of most trains bang from side to side as they roll along the tracks.

The secret of the APT is that British scientists invented a flanged wheel that rolls with perfect stability. The wheels

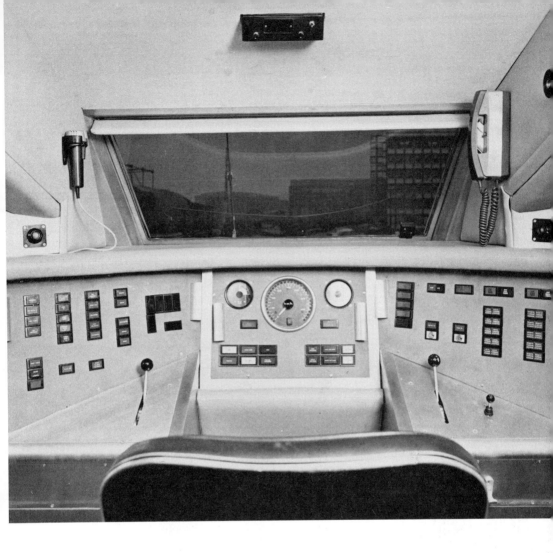

of the APT do not bang from side to side with violent contact. Its smooth-running wheels allow the APT to run on existing tracks at speeds up to 155 miles per hour.

The driver's cab of the APT is shown in the photo above. Imagine that you are in the driver's seat. There is a good view through the windshield of the cab. Three instrument dials are located on the central panel. About four dozen push switches are positioned on the side panels. The lever at your left operates the brakes. The power lever is to your right. Are you ready to go?

2

In France

The French National Railroads began adding newly designed trains long before the fuel crisis of 1974. The French are very proud of their trains. And they have good reason to be!

Train Number One of the French National Railroads is called the *Mistral*. Its run is from Paris to Nice on the Riviera. The Mistral makes the 676-mile trip in nine hours. Passengers watch the landscape whiz by at ninety-five miles per hour.

The ride on this supertrain is wonderfully smooth. The jointed track that used to make trains go clickety-clack has been replaced by welded rails. The welded sections of track up to a mile long are really without joints. Each welded joint is polished until it disappears.

It is, however, the luxury enjoyed on board the Mistral that makes it so distinctive. A twenty-four-foot long bar serves light meals. Beyond the long bar is a small shop. Perfume, newspapers, and books can be bought at the shop. There is a hairdressing salon on board, too. Both men and women are served by the hairdresser.

The doors between the coaches on the Mistral slide open automatically as a passenger approaches. In the photo above, the person is leaving what is called a *central corridor car*. Americans refer to central corridor cars as *parlor cars*. Europeans call these cars *Pullmans*.

There are also side corridor cars on the Mistral. As the name indicates, a corridor is on one side of the car. There are compartments—each with six seats—on the other side. A sliding glass door separates a compartment from the corridor.

The wide, high windows of the Mistral can be seen in the photograph of the dining car. Double panes of glass protect the air-conditioned atmosphere of the train. Between the double panes of glass is a venetian blind. The blinds are operated electrically. A push on a button raises or lowers the blind as you wish. Another button tilts the vanes of the venetian blind up or down.

Six-course dinners are available in the dining car. Passengers can also be served meals at their seats either in the central or side corridor cars. Built into the wall alongside each group of seats is a table that unfolds at mealtime. Stewards serve meals to the passengers from the kitchen of the dining car.

3

The Turbotrains
of France

The French Railways put a lot of effort into making the passenger comfortable. Their routes also make it convenient to travel from the center of one city to the center of another. The French are attempting to combine comfort and convenience with swifter rail transportation.

Some years ago the aerospace industry developed lightweight gas turbines for helicopters and light propeller-driven aircraft. The French were among the first to recognize the importance of the gas turbine as a means of propulsion for trains. They were the first in the world with a fully successful, trouble-free service of gas turbine-powered trains.

Some of the first-generation gas turbines used by the French weighed a mere three and three-fourths tons. This included about one and one-half tons of sound insulation. A modern diesel engine of the same power output weighs about thirteen tons. The French gas turbines produce a lot of power in relation to their weight.

A multiple-unit diesel produces a maximum speed of about 100 miles per hour. A multiple-unit gas turbine, however, can operate at 150 miles per hour. A complete gas turbine-powered train weighs less and actually costs less to operate than a diesel-powered train.

Initially, people thought that gas turbine-powered trains would produce a lot of noise pollution. Careful attention to insulation of the engine compartment, however, reduces the noise pollution significantly. Proper design of the air intake and exhaust of the gas-turbine engine also helps to reduce noise. With proper insulation and design, a gas turbine-powered train generates less noise than a diesel.

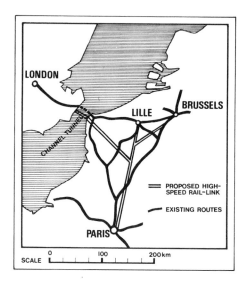

The French plan to build a new high-speed railway from Paris to Lille. Original plans called for turbotrains to run along this route at speeds up to 185 miles per hour.

But because of the energy crisis, the French are taking a long, hard look at their turbotrains. The running costs of an electrified system may be much less. The French are trying to decide whether to use electric or turbo service.

There are plans to build a tunnel under the English Channel. The tunnel will connect France and Great Britain. A branch of the Paris-Lille high-speed line will have its terminal at the channel tunnel.

High-speed rail service will reduce London-Paris travel time to two and three-fourths hours. This compares favorably with the time spent traveling from city center to city center by air.

4

In Japan

In October 1964, the Japanese National Railways opened a new two-track railway line between Tokyo and Shin-Osaka. The Japanese refer to this line as the *Shinkansen*.

High-speed trains such as the Hikari shown in the photograph are in service on the new line. These trains flash along the Shinkansen at 125 miles per hour. The 318-mile trip between Tokyo and Shin-Osaka takes about four hours.

The trains that run on the tracks of the Shinkansen are almost totally automatic. Each train is operated remotely from control centers in the terminal cities. An engineer in the cab of the train tends only to whatever manual maneuvering the train requires.

The extension of the Shinkansen from Shin-Osaka to Okayama—a distance of 100 miles—was opened in March 1972. The last section of the line from Okayama to Hakata —a distance of about 250 miles—was opened in 1975.

The Japanese spent a lot of money to build the Shinkansen. But it has been worth it! On the average, about one quarter of a million people travel on the Shinkansen each day. On some days, more than one-half million people travel on these high-speed trains. The passenger fares more than pay the cost of operating the line.

The number of people using the Shinkansen has been increasing each year. In order to deal with the increasing traffic, the Japanese National Railways is increasing the number and length of the trains. For example, at the time of its opening there were thirty round trips per day on the Shinkansen. Today, however, there are well over one hundred round trips per day. And the number of cars on all Hikari trains has been increased to sixteen.

Three other Shinkansen lines from Tokyo are being built. One of these lines runs from Tokyo to Narita Airport. Another runs from Tokyo to Niigata. The third Shinkansen being built runs from Tokyo to Morioka. Each of these new Shinkansen lines is scheduled for completion in 1977.

The Japanese National Railways has a good safety record. The Shinkansen rail cars undergo a very careful inspection after every nineteen thousand miles of operation. The roadbed is built strong and sturdy for high-speed train operation. Every mile of track is inspected at least every ten days.

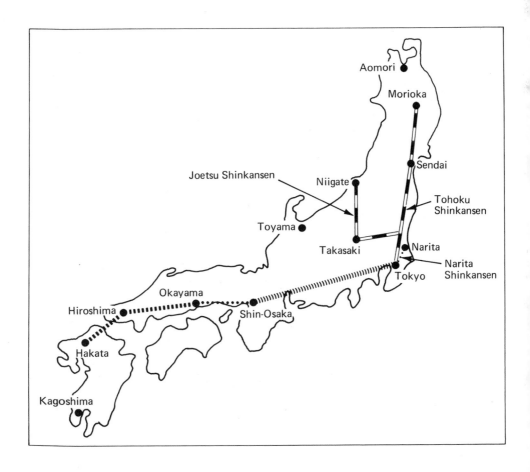

5

A Flying
Railroad

The Shinkansen from Tokyo to Hakata is called the *Tokaido Shinkansen*. The present Tokaido line should reach the limit of its capacity around 1980. This estimate is based on the carrying capacity of the trains and how fast they can travel.

In other words, Japanese planners are saying that by 1980 there will be as many trains as possible moving over the Shinkansen tracks from Tokyo to Hakata. But they foresee that there will be more passengers waiting to board than can be carried by the trains. If nothing is done the Japanese will be facing a severe problem.

The Japanese answer to the problem is to build a second Tokaido Shinkansen. On the second line the Japanese plan to operate magnetic trains. The experimental model of the Japanese magnetic train is shown in the photo. It is capable of moving just above the ground at speeds of three hundred miles per hour.

The secret of the swift silent ride is simple magnetism. Superconducting coils in the vehicle induce electric currents in the track bed coils. The magnetic repulsion produced by these electric currents is used to suspend and guide the vehicle. The train is actually lifted and propelled forward by strong electromagnetic forces.

The Japanese plan to place a supermagnetic train in service for the 318-mile ride between Tokyo and Osaka by 1980. The travel time for the trip will be about one hour.

6

In Canada

In some ways Canada is unique. It is a large country with a relatively small population. This combination may account for the fact that the railway passenger business in Canada is in deep trouble. About 85 per cent of intercity travelers now move by private automobile.

The Canadian Government recognizes that railway passenger services do, in fact, lose money. But the government is satisfied there is a continuing need for many of these services. Therefore, the Canadian Government has offered to pay up to 80 per cent of the losses on passenger trains which are considered vital to Canada.

The Canadian National Railways System has shown some interest in new transportation technology. But the introduction of turbotrains has not been very successful. In the spring of 1973, for example, CN placed turbotrains back into service for the fourth time in five years on the Montreal-Toronto run.

The engines in the newly modified CN turbotrain have been proven in more than ten million flying hours as power plants for aircraft. Five engines are aboard each of the three CN turbotrains. Four of the engines are used for traction. The fifth engine supplies power for the services —electricity and air conditioning, for example—on the train.

Canadian National's turbotrain makes the 335-mile run between Montreal and Toronto in about four hours. The average speed on the run—including stops—is eighty-four miles per hour. Canada's most heavily populated corridor is between Montreal and Toronto. So this run should give CN's turbotrain its best chance for success.

One of the big problems, however, is that CN has placed turbotrains on its old rails. A turbotrain needs to run on welded rails. Freight trains are running over the same track, too. The freight trains beat down the roadbed and slow the movement of the turbotrains.

On the run between Montreal and Toronto, there are three hundred grade crossings. This fact alone makes it very difficult to maintain safety. On one of its first runs, the CN turbotrain hit a truck on one of the grade crossings. In order to have truly modern railway passenger service, the Canadians must be willing to make a lot of changes and spend a lot of money.

In the past, railroads played a major role in the development of Canada. They helped push the frontier westward. And the railroads made it possible to open the resources of the country to development. Railroads also contributed to the concentration of activities in urban areas. Most of the time, for example, towns just grew up around the railroad station.

The railways of yesteryear made great contributions because they were using the best technology of the times and applying it in creative ways to meet needs that existed. Today, however, most of the Canadian effort is simply directed to improving services on existing facilities. The existing facilities are old. This is not the way progress is made!

The provincial government is playing the same game. The government of Ontario, for example, operates the GO Transport System. It covers a fifty-nine-mile stretch along existing CN tracks from Hamilton in the west through Toronto to Pickering in the east along Lake Ontario.

The GO uses reasonably modern equipment. Two of the self-propelled commuter cars can be seen in the photograph. The service is reasonably fast. It has attracted some commuters back to the tracks. The commuter service, however, does operate at a loss.

Rapid Transit, U. S. A.

During the last ten years the federal government has spent one hundred times more money for highways than for mass transit. We see the evidence of how the money was spent all around. Ribbons of concrete crisscross the countryside. And we have had a concrete invasion of superhighways into the very heart of our cities.

Cities like Houston, Texas, and Los Angeles, California, have grown and sprawled within the last thirty years. Main roads were widened and new roads were built. But for all practical purposes there is no mass transit system in either city.

In fact, the mass transit system that Los Angeles had was dismantled. Great quantities of asphalt and concrete were spread across the land. Eventually, more than 50 per cent of Los Angeles was covered by asphalt and concrete.

Some people insist that more and more highway construction is needed. Others say there is a better way. The better way is through mass rapid transit!

7

Cities Must Decide

Basically, the residents of an area must determine the type of city they want. They cannot leave this decision to others. All transportation planning should be directed toward fulfilling their goals.

The citizens of San Francisco, for example, want to preserve the unique character of their city. The cable car is a colorful part of the heritage of San Francisco. The cable car also happens to be very useful in moving people up and down the hills of San Francisco.

In the photograph at the top of the page, riders are helping to change the direction of a cable car on the Powell Street turntable. Immediately below the cable car turntable is the underground Powell Street station of BART, a rapid rail system. The sign on the platform in the lower photo indicates that the next BART train is heading toward Daly City. The citizens of San Francisco want a colorful city with all its traditions as well as the convenience of rapid rail transit.

8

The Metro Areas

Today there are at least forty-one metropolitan areas in the United States large enough to support well-developed mass-rapid transit systems. In some of these cities systems exist. In others, little or nothing is being done to develop rapid transit.

On the Pacific Coast we have the metropolitan areas of Seattle, Portland, San Francisco, Los Angeles, and San Diego. Among them, San Francisco stands alone in its attempt to establish rapid transit.

Phoenix, Arizona, and Denver, Colorado, qualify as large urban areas. Texas has Fort Worth, Dallas, Houston, and San Antonio. The most imaginative planning for moving people in these cities is at the Dallas-Fort Worth Regional Airport.

The system at the Dallas-Fort Worth Airport is called *Airtrans*. It consists of a vehicle and guideway network. The system is designed to move passengers rapidly, comfortably, and safely.

Each forty-passenger vehicle in the Airtrans system is powered by electricity. The entire system is under the control of a single operator sitting at a central console. The system covers a total distance of thirteen miles.

As we move into the heartland of our country, we find the metropolitan areas of Minneapolis, St. Paul, Kansas City, St. Louis, Memphis, Louisville, Cincinnati, Columbus, and Indianapolis. All of these areas need balanced transportation systems. The automobile is still king in all of them. They are "car happy" cities.

Along the Great Lakes, the large metropolitan areas are Milwaukee, Chicago, Cleveland, and Buffalo. Chicago and Cleveland have rapid transit systems. Cleveland was the first city in the United States with a rapid transit system serving a major airport.

In our southern states, the large urban areas capable of supporting rapid transit are New Orleans, Miami, St. Petersburg-Tampa, Jacksonville, Atlanta, and Birmingham. Among these, only the Atlanta area is moving toward the development of a balanced mass transportation system.

As we move northward, we come to Washington, D.C.— our nation's capital. A ninety-eight-mile rapid rail transit system was authorized by Congress and approved by the voters of the region. The system is called *Metro*.

The map shows the areas serviced by Metro. A small portion of the system was opened in 1974. The plan is to have the whole system in operation by 1979.

In the circular insert of the map on page 37, you can identify the Metro stations within the District of Columbia. Move westward across the Potomac River to find the Rosslyn, Virginia, and the Pentagon stations. The Metro transit routes fork at these stations.

REGIONAL RAPID RAIL TRANSIT SYSTEM

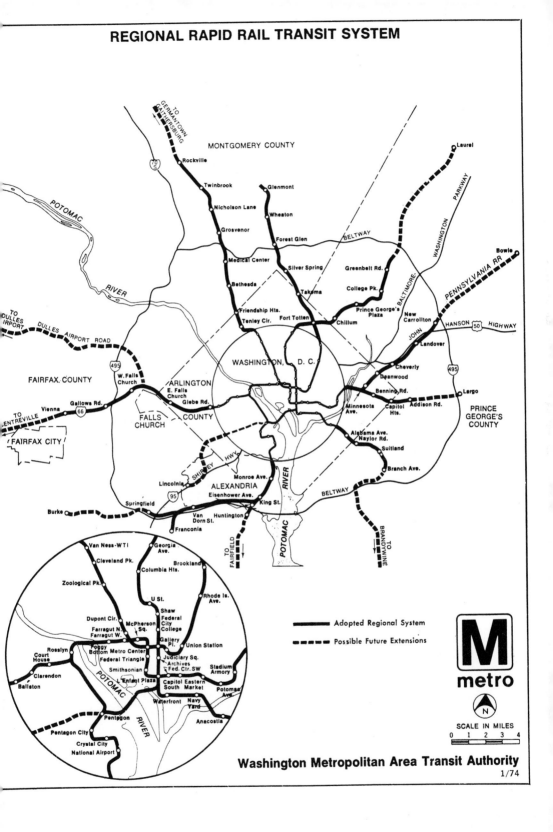

Washington Metropolitan Area Transit Authority
1/74

The Rosslyn and Pentagon stations are bilevel stations. A bilevel station is shown in the illustration on the opposite page. Outgoing and incoming trains arrive on different levels. This arrangement permits one train to go under the tracks of the other. The different levels eliminate the need for a grade crossing. This is one way to build safety into the system. Passengers use escalators to transfer from one platform to another. A bilevel station represents good planning.

Thus far, we have identified thirty-four cities large enough to support mass transit systems. Pittsburgh—northwest of Washington, D.C.—is another city in need of good mass transit. Northeast of Washington, D.C., there are six large urban areas: Baltimore, the South Jersey region, Philadelphia, New York City, Providence, and Boston. All have systems in operation that need improvement.

What is needed, however, is for the citizens in each of the forty-one large urban areas of the United States to take a good look at their regions. Are they satisfied with the transportation systems available to them? Do the systems presently in use pollute the environment and create excessive noise?

9

Balanced Transportation

The best solution to metropolitan travel problems is, of course, a balanced transportation system. The term "balanced transportation" means a coordinated network of high-speed rail transit, automobiles on expressways, feeder buses, and outlying parking facilities. Each mode of transport in such a network is used to do the job it does best.

In the metropolitan area of New York City, a balanced transportation system is in the process of being developed. At the present time, parking facilities exist in New Jersey close to the western end of the Lincoln Tunnel. People drive from outlying areas in New Jersey by automobile to the parking facilities. After parking their cars, they board buses which take them through the Lincoln Tunnel to the Port Authority Bus Terminal. At the terminal, they can board subways or buses to their final destinations in New York City.

From Connecticut, passengers board the Cosmopolitans
—new commuter cars designed to give a safe, on-time ride
to and from New York's Grand Central Station. The Cosmopolitans shown in the photo are electric self-propelled
cars which operate in pairs. They are capable of speeds up
to one hundred miles per hour. Wide-contoured seats on
these trains add to passenger comfort. Soft carpeting and air

conditioning contribute to the luxury of the ride. After arriving at Grand Central Station, the traveler can board a subway or bus to reach his final destination.

The Port Authority of New York and New Jersey operates a rapid-rail transit system called *PATH*. The present rail system is about fourteen miles long. It provides frequent service between stations in New Jersey and New York City. The PATH trains move into New York City through under-river tunnels.

The map of the current and proposed PATH system identifies the areas served. PATH is a primary transit link between New York City and neighboring New Jersey communities. The extension of the service to Plainfield will allow passengers to travel to Newark International Airport by rail. The PATH extension is part of a broad program of public transportation improvements planned for New Jersey and New York.

PATH also provides a link between New York City and suburban commuter railroads. The Penn Central, Central of New Jersey, Reading, and Amtrak railroads connect with PATH at its Newark station. The Erie Lackawanna Railway connects with PATH at its Hoboken station. PATH carries over 70 per cent of all passengers entering New York City by rail from New Jersey.

The PATH Journal Square Transportation Center shown on page 43 is located in the commercial and shopping center of Jersey City—New Jersey's second largest city. The center includes a rapid-rail transit station, a terminal for buses serving thirty routes, and a parking area for over six hundred cars. Improved transportation services result from the coordination of rapid rail transit with feeder buses and autos.

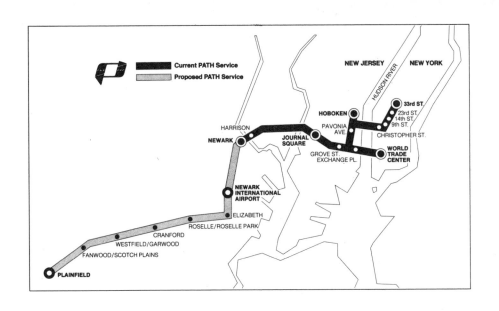

Current PATH Service
Proposed PATH Service

NEW JERSEY   NEW YORK

HUDSON RIVER

33rd ST.
23rd ST.
14th ST.
9th ST.
CHRISTOPHER ST.

HOBOKEN

PAVONIA AVE.

HARRISON

NEWARK   JOURNAL SQUARE

GROVE ST.
EXCHANGE PL.

WORLD TRADE CENTER

NEWARK INTERNATIONAL AIRPORT

ELIZABETH

ROSELLE/ROSELLE PARK

CRANFORD

WESTFIELD/GARWOOD

FANWOOD/SCOTCH PLAINS

PLAINFIELD

Whenever balanced transportation is discussed we need to mention Chicago. Metropolitan Chicago was one of the first urban centers to plan for balanced transportation. The Chicago Transit Authority was established by legislative action and approved by the voters of Chicago in 1945.

The CTA has done an excellent job of operating and coordinating bus routes and rapid rail transit. But the most farsighted undertaking of the CTA was to place rapid rail lines in the center mall of Chicago's highways. In the photograph, a CTA train is moving along the median strip of the Kennedy Expressway.

44

The first expressway in Chicago to have rapid-rail transit facilities installed on the center mall was the Eisenhower Expressway. Almost 200,000 automobiles travel east and west over the 15½-mile stretch of this expressway from downtown Chicago to suburban Hillside during any weekday. During peak travel hours, the trains that run on the center mall carry about 50 per cent more people than the four-lane expressways.

Using the center mall of expressways for high-speed rail transport puts land to good use. There is no need to "grab" more land for new right of ways. This kind of land use also keeps construction costs as low as possible.

The Eisenhower Expressway is an east-west corridor that leads to downtown Chicago. The addition of rapid rail lines on the center mall increases its passenger-carrying capacity. The high-speed rail line of the Eisenhower Expressway actually increases its passenger-carrying capacity by 500 per cent.

Balanced transportation for a metropolitan area also means good connections with the airports that serve the region. Dulles International Airport is located twenty-six miles west of Washington, D.C. Present ground transportation to the airport causes frustrating delays. As a result, the airport is not being used to its best advantage.

An aerial transport system has been suggested as a way of linking Dulles Airport and downtown Washington. The system resembles a monorail. It can carry passengers at speeds up to a hundred miles per hour.

The track is supported from thin columns called *pylons*. The pylons occupy a minimum of ground space. The system can be built in the airspace over congested areas and along the median strips of expressways.

There are no smog-producing exhaust fumes from the system. It is operated by electricity. The vehicles run on pneumatic tires along the enclosed beamway. Thus, the system is quiet.

The track is enclosed and will stay dry under all conditions. Since the system is elevated, snow and other forms of precipitation will not impede the travel of the vehicles. The system can operate in all kinds of weather.

10

Impact on the Environment

San Francisco's Bay Area Rapid Transit system is called *BART*. The seventy-five-mile system is a regional rapid transit network. BART serves San Francisco, Alameda, and Contra Costa counties.

All of man's activities affect our environment. BART has an impact on the environment in four ways: energy consumption, noise production, air pollution, and the use of land.

Before BART, most of the people in the area traveled by automobile. We need to conserve our dwindling energy resources. One way to conserve is to make the most efficient use of our available supplies. A rapid rail system conserves energy through efficient use.

BART trains do make noise. But careful attention to tracks, cars, and stations reduces noise to a minimum. In fact, a BART train makes much less noise than a typical diesel truck or normal freeway traffic.

48

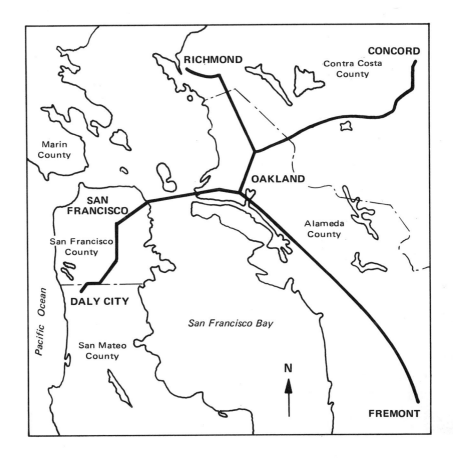

The BART track is mounted on rubber dampeners. It is also welded, which does away with the clickety-clack sound. Side skirts on the cars are used to muffle noise that is unavoidable. Skillful use of acoustical materials in stations helps to absorb sound. A BART train can glide into a subway station without disturbing your conversation.

BART is an electric system. It produces no pollution of its own as it glides along its track. BART's passengers, however, formerly used automobiles. If BART were not available they would all be driving. Before BART, its passengers drove a cumulative total of 600,000 miles per day. This kind of driving sent almost fourteen tons of pollutants into the air each day.

A government has the right to take private property for public use. This right is called *eminent domain.* Government planners are required by law to exercise this right very cautiously and carefully.

The BART system includes twenty-three miles of underground and underwater construction. Aerial construction accounts for twenty-five miles of track. Another twenty-seven miles of the BART right of way was built along existing or proposed transportation corridors. Most of the four miles of new corridor space required for BART was in the industrial West Oakland area.

In some areas it was necessary to widen the right of way for BART. A total of six miles of housing was taken and destroyed to make way for the project. It is, of course, unfortunate when housing is destroyed to build lines and stations.

There are a sufficient number of stations on the present seventy-five-mile route to make its use convenient. In the photograph, passengers at the MacArthur station are waiting to board a train that will travel to Fremont. A glance at the system map shows that the passengers may be traveling to eleven different stations along this section of the route.

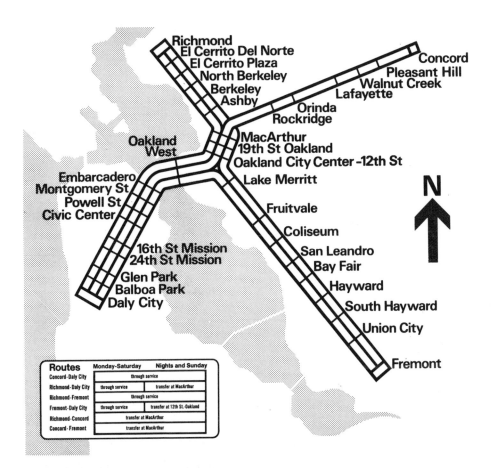

Richmond
El Cerrito Del Norte
El Cerrito Plaza
North Berkeley
Berkeley
Ashby

Concord
Pleasant Hill
Walnut Creek
Lafayette
Orinda
Rockridge

Oakland
West

MacArthur
19th St Oakland
Oakland City Center -12th St

Embarcadero
Montgomery St
Powell St
Civic Center

Lake Merritt

Fruitvale

Coliseum

San Leandro
Bay Fair

Hayward

South Hayward

Union City

Fremont

16th St Mission
24th St Mission
Glen Park
Balboa Park
Daly City

N

Routes	Monday-Saturday	Nights and Sunday
Concord-Daly City	through service	
Richmond-Daly City	through service	transfer at MacArthur
Richmond-Fremont	through service	
Fremont-Daly City	through service	transfer at 12th St.-Oakland
Richmond-Concord	transfer at MacArthur	
Concord-Fremont	transfer at MacArthur	

11

Amtrak

The National Railroad Passenger Corporation was created by Congress in 1970. This government-backed system has been nicknamed Amtrak. The job of Amtrak is to unify, improve, and run intercity passenger service in the United States.

From its birth, Amtrak has directed a lot of attention to the region that stretches from Washington, D.C., to Boston. This area is densely populated and heavily traveled. It is called the *Northeast Corridor.*

The distance from Washington through New York to Boston is 450 miles. There are twelve major cities along the Northeast Corridor. Moving northeast from Washington, D.C., we find Baltimore, Wilmington, Philadelphia, Trenton, New Brunswick, Newark, New York, Bridgeport, New Haven, Providence, and Boston.

The distance between cities along the Northeast Corridor is not great. With one-hundred- and three-hundred-mile links between cities, high-speed trains can compete with airplanes. Amtrak's sleek high-speed Metroliner, for example, makes the run between New York and Washington in two and one-half hours. When you consider your door-to-door travel time, a train may, in fact, be faster than a plane for such a trip.

Each Metroliner car is powered by electricity. The train is computer controlled and almost automatic. The operator uses only one control to dial the speed desired. The Metroliner is capable of traveling at 120 miles per hour. Metroliner service offers fifteen round trips on weekdays between New York and Washington, D.C.

There are a number of metropolitan centers in the United States that are separated by distances of one hundred to three hundred miles. In addition to the New York-Washington link, there are New York-Boston, Chicago-Milwaukee, and San Diego-Los Angeles links that are favorable for high-speed rail service.

On January 25, 1971, Metroliner service was linked with high-speed turbotrain service for the New York to Boston run. Amtrak's turbotrains are powered by airplane gas-turbine engines. Amtrak's first turbotrains were purchased from the French.

Amtrak's trains running between metropolitan centers separated by distances of three hundred miles can do something that airplanes cannot do well. The high-speed train can take care of all those people who are not going from one big metropolitan center to another. A high-speed train is the best mode of travel for all those people traveling somewhere in-between. Along the Northeast Corridor, for example, some people may travel from Washington to Baltimore, others may get on at Wilmington, and some passengers may have Philadelphia as their destination.

When we study the transportation needs of our people we become aware of many problems: Airways and highways are getting more crowded. Railroad right of ways are getting very little use. There are many people in various parts

of the country who cannot be served really well by airlines. And they are not being served by trains either.

We really should be thinking of ways in which railroads and airlines can work together. We have placed too much importance on competition and not enough on cooperation. We must make the best and most efficient means of transportation available to the citizens of the United States.

12

Personal Rapid Transit

Morgantown, West Virginia, like a lot of American cities, suffers from traffic congestion, noise, and air pollution. The traffic problems of Morgantown are made more difficult by three widely separated campuses of West Virginia University. Five times a day, more than one thousand students move from one campus to another for classes.

A computer-operated, small-car Personal Rapid Transit system, called *PRT,* was installed in Morgantown in 1972. The system connects the city's central business district and the three campuses of West Virginia University.

A passenger boarding a PRT vehicle selects his destination by pushing a button. When the doors slide shut, the vehicle goes directly to the station selected. In some ways the system operates like an elevator.

In the past, moving students by bus or auto caused traffic to reach peak levels every hour on weekdays. The short auto trip across town sometimes took as much as an hour. PRT reduced the between-campus travel time to five minutes.

With all its advantages the PRT is in trouble—money trouble! The cost of the experiment jumped from $13 million to $115 million. By April 1974, the federal government was saying that the system cost too much and should be closed down.

The PRT system at Morgantown ran out of money. But it may still point the way to the future. In the City of Tomorrow, air-polluting traffic can be denied entry. Private autos, taxis, and buses can be replaced by PRT systems operating on guideways.

In the meantime, we also need to find ways to redesign our present cities to relieve congestion and pollution. We can, for example, build parking facilities outside the central business districts. PRT systems can be used to move people from the parking facilities to the business centers. The central areas of cities can be turned into pedestrian malls.

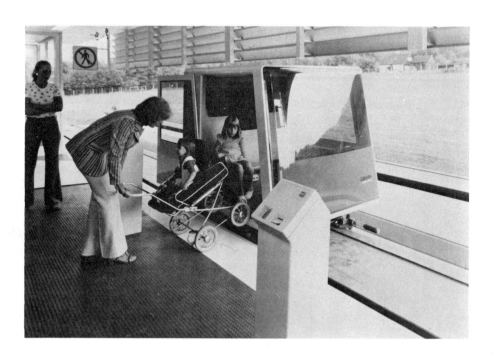

UNIT 3

Transit Systems for the Future

Automobiles and aircraft have the capacity for random and practically trackless travel, although today airliners are required to follow "tracks in the sky." An airliner is assigned an air corridor in which it flies from one point to another. Automobiles, too, are not allowed to wander randomly across the countryside. They must travel along roads which are, in a sense, their tracks.

The success of the auto and the airplane in this century stifled the progress of special-purpose track systems such as trains. But the congestion along highways and airways focuses new attention on special-purpose track systems.

Today, scientists are attempting to develop high-speed ground systems to carry passengers at three hundred miles per hour. Conventional rails are not suitable at these speeds. Noncontact suspensions—air or magnetic—seem to be the practical solutions.

13

Magnetic Trains

Magnets of like polarity repel each other. Those of unlike polarity attract. Magnetic suspensions can use either an attractive or a repulsive magnetic force. Most experimental vehicles of today use repulsive forces.

The first full-scale magnetic vehicle in the world was developed by MBB-International of Germany in 1971. The vehicle in the photo was used to test magnetic suspension, guidance, and propulsion techniques.

The new magnetic field technology does away with contact between rail and vehicle. This offers the possibility of operating these vehicles at very high speeds.

The length of the test track for the MBB experimental vehicle was 2,165 feet. As the vehicle hurtles along it makes use of electromagnets to suspend the vehicle and for lateral guidance. These electromagnets are controlled in such a way that an air gap is always maintained between the vehicle and the guidance rail. The car floats about one-fourth of an inch above its magnetic track.

A special type of electric motor, called a *linear induction motor*, moves the vehicle down the track. It is also used to brake the vehicle. The linear motor produces electromagnetic fields. The forked-shaped motor straddles an aluminum reaction rail that is fixed to the track. In the photograph, we are looking head-on at the aluminum reaction rail.

The linear induction motor has no mechanically moving parts. It is a nonrotating electric drive. This is in sharp contrast to the usual rotary electric motor which has bearings and rotating commutators.

The magnetic suspension technique and the linear motor drive are both based on the effects of magnetic fields. Thus we have a vehicle with no mechanical contact to the rail. This keeps noise levels low. And since we are dealing with electromagnetic fields, the vehicle does not produce air-fouling substances.

Magnetic trains of the future will give smooth, quiet rides. They will also be noise free. And these magnetic trains will push land travel to three hundred miles per hour.

14

The French Aerotrains

The idea of building an air-cushion guide vehicle was the subject of patents in Great Britain and France in 1962. But a French company, Bertin, was the first to promote successfully the air-cushion train. The efforts of Bertin led to the incorporation in France of the Société de l'Aérotrain. Since 1965, this French group has been actively engaged in testing and developing this type of transportation system.

The Aerotrain I-80, called the *Orléans*, was built in 1969. For more than two years this aerotrain was tested on an eleven-mile elevated track near Orléans. The vehicle is supported by a cushion of air and driven by a rear propeller. It carries 80 passengers at a cruising speed of 165 miles per hour.

In January 1973, the Orléans was equipped with a new high-speed propulsion system shown opposite below. This new system drives the vehicle at speeds of 250 miles per hour. A new test program began during the summer of 1973, and was conducted on the same eleven-mile-long elevated guideway near Orléans.

Aerotrain S-44 was built in 1969 and tested on a track in Gometz. The vehicle shown in the photo below was designed to carry forty-four passengers. It is powered by a linear induction motor. The support and guiding systems are air cushions supplied by two ventilators.

The French are working toward an all-electric aerotrain. The ventilators on some newer models operate with standard electric motors. In fact, they have found that sufficient air is trapped to maintain the support cushions when cruising at high speeds. Thus, the whole system can work on its own. The uplift is apparently provided free.

The full-scale tests of experimental aerotrains were very encouraging. By 1971, the French Government had developed much confidence in its aerotrains. And it decided to build the first commercial aerotrain line in the world. The fifteen-mile line was to link the new business center of Paris-La Défense with the new town of Cergy-Pontoise.

A new vehicle shown above was being designed for this service. However, the estimated costs to build the system doubled in three years. This led the French Government to cancel the building of the line in July 1974.

The Société de l'Aérotrain is a private company. And it is continuing its experiments to develop a linear induction motor to propel a new aerotrain at speeds over 150 miles per hour. In the new model, the cars—supported by low-pressure cushions of air—will straddle an aluminum rail. The aluminum rail is set in a concrete guideway. It will act both to guide the vehicle and as a motor-reaction rail.

Bertin, the inventor of the aerotrain, still believes that it is well suited to interurban service between cities 60 to 250 miles apart. Aerotrain runs could be frequent between such locations. Rapid city-center to city-center transportation could be made available by the use of aerotrains.

Aerotrain guideways can be built along the median strip of expressways. They, of course, can also be built along the sides of existing highways. Placing aerotrains in such locations would eliminate the need to condemn land for the right of way. It would reduce the costs involved in constructing the system, too.

15

The TMT Monorail

An elevated monorail has been designed by Marty Trent at North American Rockwell. The system has been named *Tri-Mono-Trans,* or *TMT* for short.

As designed, the vehicle is capable of a three-hundred-mile-per-hour cruising speed. The over-all length of the TMT vehicle is 116 feet. It can carry 204 passengers.

Two passenger fuselages hang on either side of the track from a center fuselage. This gives the vehicle a low center of gravity. Since the center of gravity is below the guideway surface, it has great stability.

The passenger carriages are 11 feet in diameter. The center fuselage is about 14 feet wide. On the lower portion of the center fuselage is the running surface which moves along the convex-shaped guideway. The guideway support pillars are spaced about 50 feet apart.

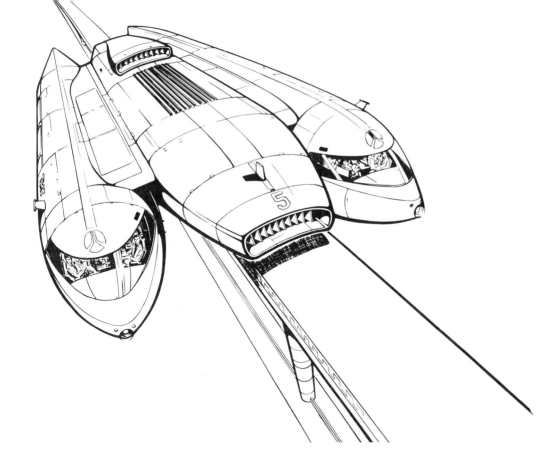

AIRLINE TYPE PASSENGER ACCOMMODATIONS

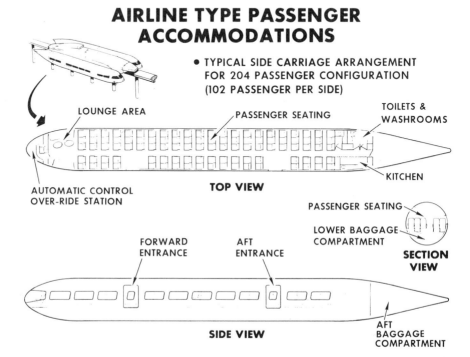

- TYPICAL SIDE CARRIAGE ARRANGEMENT FOR 204 PASSENGER CONFIGURATION (102 PASSENGER PER SIDE)

LOUNGE AREA

PASSENGER SEATING

TOILETS & WASHROOMS

KITCHEN

AUTOMATIC CONTROL OVER-RIDE STATION

TOP VIEW

PASSENGER SEATING

LOWER BAGGAGE COMPARTMENT

SECTION VIEW

FORWARD ENTRANCE

AFT ENTRANCE

SIDE VIEW

AFT BAGGAGE COMPARTMENT

COMPACT STATION FACILITIES FOR NEAR TERM URBAN INSTALLATION

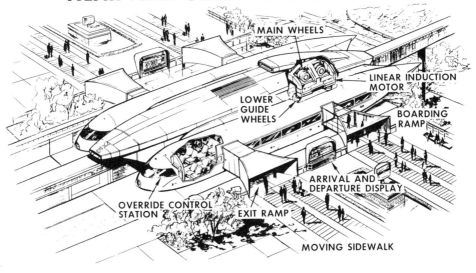

MAIN WHEELS

LINEAR INDUCTION MOTOR

LOWER GUIDE WHEELS

BOARDING RAMP

ARRIVAL AND DEPARTURE DISPLAY

OVERRIDE CONTROL STATION

EXIT RAMP

MOVING SIDEWALK

The TMT vehicle is powered by a linear induction motor. In a linear induction motor the coils and armature are laid flat. The track itself becomes a long armature. The field coils are built into the train. When alternating current is put into the track, the field coils are repelled. They move in a linear direction down the track and pull the vehicle with them.

In order for the linear induction motor to propel the vehicle efficiently, the track and train must not touch. The running surface of the center fuselage is kept about an inch or so off the six-foot-wide track. The separation is maintained with wheels at low speed and air pressure at high speed.

From standstill to about a hundred miles per hour, the center fuselage rides on rubber tires. Inside the hollow center fuselage, four electrically driven air compressors work to build the air pressure. As the air cushion builds, the rubber tires retract and the craft glides along on the air cushion.

At three hundred miles per hour, the air being rammed into the scoop of the center fuselage is sufficient to supply the lift. At this cruising speed, the air compressors can idle. They are not necessary to supply the air-cushion system.

16

A Tube Train

In 1971, a patent was granted for a tube transportation system. The system uses a steel-lined concrete tube. The new idea is to let steam push an entire train through the tube.

The pollution-free system could propel a train at four hundred miles per hour. The train is sent on its way by the build-up of steam pressure behind it. As the train moves, it rams into lower pressure steam, which will condense. The liquid vaporizes again when the vehicle passes because a partial vacuum is produced behind the moving train.

Stanford scientists are working on another way to run a high-speed train inside a tube. They are designing a tube vehicle to be propelled by a supercooled electromagnet.

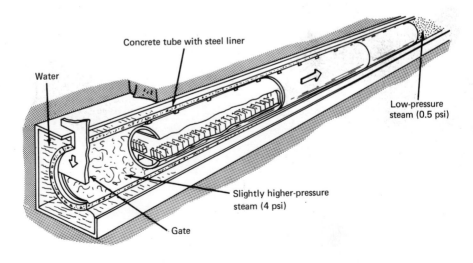

Concrete tube with steel liner

Water

Low-pressure steam (0.5 psi)

Slightly higher-pressure steam (4 psi)

Gate

Photo Credits

Amtrak, pp. 52, 55
BART, pp. 30, 48, 51
Boeing Corporation, pp. 56, 57
British Railways Board, pp. 11, 13
Celeste Navarra, p. 33
Chicago Transit Authority, p. 45
French National Railroads, pp. 15, 16, 17, 19, 20
General Electric, pp. 40, 47
Hawker-Siddley, Canada, Ltd., p. 29
Japanese National Railways, pp. 21, 23, 25
LITVAC, p. 34
Messerschmitt-Bölkow-Blohm, pp. 58, 63, 65
North American Rockwell, pp. 71, 72, 73, 74
Otis Elevator, p. 59
The Port Authority of New York, pp. 8, 43, 44
Sante Fe Railway, pp. 2, 12
Société Bertin et Cie, pp. 66, 68, 69
Société de l'Aérotrain, p. 67
United Aircraft Corporation, pp. 6, 27
U. S. Department of Transportation, p. 60
Washington Metropolitan Area Transit Authority, pp. 37, 39

Index

77

About the Author

JOHN GABRIEL NAVARRA, the author of *Supertrains,* is professor of geoscience and was, for ten years, chairman of the division of science at Jersey City State College. As both a teacher and a writer, Dr. Navarra has an international reputation. He was the teacher of the first televised science course to be offered in the South when he was on the faculty of East Carolina University. He has written a number of trade books for young readers as well as adult science books, and he is the senior author of a complete series of science textbooks, grades kindergarten through nine, that are used by millions of schoolchildren throughout the United States.